ROCKET AROUND *Switzerland!*
A neurodiverse-friendly storybook for kids

Written by
Lee Lynch

Illustrations
Emma Lynch

Contributors
Jeffrey, Jack, & Tom Lynch

Guest Appearance
Dottie

ROCKET AROUND LLC

This book is for neurodiverse and neurotypical kids around the world of any age, who love adventure, imagination, and finding new ways to have fun!

Neurodiverse people behave, think, and learn differently from people with neurotypical brains. These differences include strengths. In a word, neurodiverse people are awesome. Neurodiverse people might be autistic, live with ADHD, dyslexia, PTSD, Tourette's, or other things.

Safety Tips

Being safe when you travel is important. Remember to:

-Keep the adult you're with in sight
-Set a place to meet in case you cannot find your adult
-Know their phone number - write it here:_____
-If you feel lost, ask a police officer or information desk for help
-If your family has an emergency when in Switzerland, call phone number 112 (that's like 911 in the U.S.)

BE SAFE!

Everywhere We Go in This Book...

You can also see where all of the above sites are located on the map on Pg. 39

Everywhere We Go continued

See page 44 to be a ROCKETAROUNDER!

Guten tag travel friend!

Guten tag means good day in German. Why am I talking to you in German?

My neurodiverse family is going to Switzerland, and in some parts of that country, they speak German.

You remember my human family – Jeffrey, Jack, Emma, Dad, and Mom.

They've been planning this trip for a while, and it sounds awesome!

They think I'm staying with a dog sitter, but I'll just switch myself for this Rocket stuffie in Emma's backpack.

Here we go!

Phew. Made it through security and onto the airplane!

I think I'll help the flight attendants – cookies anyone?

I LOVE flying! So many fun things to do – watch movies, play games, get petted by people around me, eat, and sleep.

Now the pilot is about to land the plane in Geneva, Switzerland.

I'd better get in the backpack!

Here we are – Geneva, Switzerland. Bonjour! They speak French in this part of Switzerland because France is right across Lake Geneva from us!

Geneva is an old city – it's been around since 1 BC – that's more than two thousand years! There are so many things to do here. What's your favorite thing to do in Geneva?

Hey, isn't that the flight attendant from the airplane?

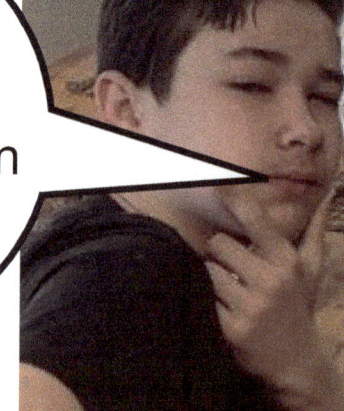

Here are my top 5 things to see in Geneva:

1. Sit (sail, or bike) along Lake Geneva and watch the humans and dogs walk by as the water jet fountain (Jet d'Eau in French) shoots water up to 450 feet (140 meters) in the air – WOW!

2. Walk around the city, from chocolate shop to chocolate shop – Swiss chocolate is the delicous!

3. Sniff the [Flower Clock in the English Garden park](#) (in French, it's called the L'horloge fleurie in the Jardin Anglais park).

4. Wander around the Medieval Old Town (in French, it's called the Vieille Ville) – a maze of narrow ancient streets.

5. Visit one of Geneva's cool museums, like the Exploracentre science center, Natural History Museum or International Museum of the Red Cross and Red Crescent.

Now – my family is on the train and heading to...

Lausanne, Switzerland - a beautiful city on the other side of Lake Geneva from Geneva.

Lausanne, like Geneva, is old About 2000 years ago, it was part of the Roman Empire, but a scary group called the Barbarians invaded, and the people who lived there ran into the nearby hills.

Ouchy Promenade

Today, Lausanne has an Old Town, which is where people lived 2000 years ago, and a New Town, in the hills.

Old Town and New Town are connected by a metro train. My humans are rocketing around Lausanne – let's follow them!

There they are – strolling along the Ouchy promenade, between the Old Harbor in the Old Town, which looks across to France.

Look, they're on those swings – wait for us!

Now they're on the move again and going into the Olympic Museum. It has stories, videos, costumes, medals, and other things from all the different Olympic Games, and it has many interactive activities for kids of all ages.

Look, Emma won a gold medal, and Dad took the silver. Go team! Now they're heading to the metro to go to the Old Town – allons-y! (let's go in French).

Olympic Museum

This metro is great – so much easier on the paws than walking up these hills. They're getting off here and heading to the Cathedrale de Lausanne – the largest Gothic-style building in Switzerland.

It sits on Cite hill, one of the three hills of the city. Now they're walking through these windy, stone streets and now down a really long staircase – market staircase (Escaliers du Marche in French).

In old days, the staircase made a path between the city's two markets. Today there are food shops and restaurants.

Cathedrale de Lausanne

Market staircase

Looks like my humans are going into a restaurant that smells like CHEESE! As you know, that's my favorite food. It's a fondue restaurant. Fondue means 'melted' in French. I've always wanted to try fondue – don't mind if I do fondue!

Have you heard of Swiss cheese?

You can get it wherever you live.

Fondue

My humans are on the move again – let's go! Looks like they're walking to the Place de la Palud.

Look – the market is open. Let's get some delicious cake, sausages and of course MORE CHEESE!

They're over at Lausanne City Hall, built 400 years ago. And right there is the Fountain of Justice, and here's the wall clock, built for the 1964 Swiss Exposition.

Sniff sniff...smells like my humans area heading toward...

Place de Palud and Fountain of Justice

Grand-Pont, which used to be called the Pont Pichard bridge. The bridge used to be two stories and about 75 feet (25 meters) high, but years ago the bottom level was covered over in dirt.

The arches remind me of a doorway. Wait, where are my humans?

Grand-Pont

Sniff sniff – smells like they've headed over to the Church of Saint Francois.

This church was first built about 900 years ago, but it burned down after only 100 years. Then it was built again into the church that stands today.

What to See - *Place Saint Francois*

The gold cobblestones in the shape of a half moon in front of the Church of St. Francis.

Each stone represents a little human born in Lausanne on a full moon night in the year 1998.

Hey, my humans have their luggage and are heading to the train station – looks like we're rocketing somewhere new! I love the train – so comfy.

The country has more than 3,000 miles of railway, and all of it runs on electricity. A lot of electricity used for Swiss trains is water-powered.

I'm just going to sneak under this seat and take a quick nap. Zzzzzzz. And now we're pulling into...

Lucerne, where they speak German. Guten tag! I can't wait to get into Old Town Lucerne– it's so cool!

My humans are strolling along the river [Reuss](), which flows into the harbor of Lake Lucerne. What a beautiful city - bridges and colorful buildings that are hundreds of years old, the harbor leading out to Mount Burgenstock, Mount Riga, and Mount Pilatus which are parts of the amazing Swiss Alps.

Old Town Lucerne

Lake Lucerne

20

Now they're heading over to Mill Square (Mühlenplatz in German) to see where the city's water wheels take flowing water and turn it into [energy for almost 1,000 houses](#).

Mill Square has had water wheels for almost 900 years!

My humans are moving on to some of Lucerne's bridges – let's go!

Old Town Lucerne has five bridges so that people can cross the river Reuss.

Mill Square

My humans are walking across the Spreuer Bridge (Spreuerbrücke in German), which has more than 45 paintings in the ceiling.

Spreuer Bridge

Chapel Bridge

They've moved onto Lucerne's most famous bridge – Chapel Bridge (Kappelbrücke in German).

It's Europe's oldest wooden bridge, and it has a small chapel in it that is almost 500 years old.

Hold on - it looks like they're heading out of Old Town to the Swiss Museum of Transport (or Verkehrshaus der Schweiz) – and why not?

There are hundreds of fun things to do here – let's do them all! Look how much fun they're having - working on a transportation project and driving the metro.

Swiss Transport Museum

Swiss Transport Museum

The Swiss Transport Museum shows and tells how different kinds of Swiss transportation work, from trains, automobiles, to ships, and aircraft. It's the most popular museum in Switzerland!

Oh geez - have to move on – looks like my humans are heading to the Port of Lucerne.

They are getting on the ferry to go to Mount Bürgenstock – jump!

Now it's just a quick trip across Lake Lucerne to Bürgenstock, a mountain we get to the top of by taking a funicular.

A funicular is a cable [railroad](#) and this one goes almost straight up a [mountainside](#).

Or you could take the road but the funicular is more fun!

Fun is even in its name!

Mount Burgenstock Funicular

Over there is another famous Lucerne site – the Musegg Wall and its nine Towers. Look how beautiful the view is!

Lake Lucerne

Hey look - it's another pup - a Bernese Mountain Dog.

They come from the Swiss Alps.

She'll know her way around here!

Hi, I'm Dottie!

26

You can look across the lake to Lucerne and into the mountains.

Wait, they're LEAVING? Come on Dottie - my humans are heading back across Lake Lucerne and I hear them saying they are going to...

Mount Pilatus – we won't want to miss that!

Mount Pilatus

What a trip - my humans took a bus, then walked up a big hill to an air gondola.

Air gondola to Mount Pilatus

An air gondola looks like an amusement ride on a cable. Now they are on a bigger air gondola.

Whoa, we just broke through the clouds!

Mount Pilatus

Mount Pilatus is right in front of us, and the Alps and the countryside is all around us! The Alps is the longest mountain range in all of Europe.

Somehow there are flags planted on the mountain by hikers and even a church!

Mount Pilatus

They look like they're in impossible places for humans to get to. I could get up there, but how would a human do it?

Fast Fact

The Alps stretches across seven countries.

Look at Jack
throwing snowballs
down Mt. Pilates
from the visitor's
center.

Glad we have our
fur on – it's cold up
here!

Time for some
selfies! Smile
Dottie!

Mount Pilatus

Pic of Rocket and Dottie!

I think we should spend some time here, hiking around, and watching the birds soar across the sky.

Mount Pilatus and Swiss Alps

Oh no, my humans are heading down the mountain. Let's go Dottie!

They're heading to the train station! Dottie, thanks for rocketing around with us - we'll see you next time we're in the Swiss Alps.

Looks like the train is pulling into [Zürich](#)! I can't wait to tour this amazing city.

They speak German here, which is gut (good in German). Everywhere you look there's a pretty site.

Limmat river

There's Lake Zürich, the Old Town which sits on both sides of the Limmat river.

All over Zürich there are colorful houses, old churches, courtyards, narrow alleys, and clocks.

City of Zurich

Fast Fact:

Zurich is the largest city in Switzerland, and it's another old place – a more than 2,000-year-old city, and people have lived here for more than 6,000 years!

And there are many places to get cheese and chocolate.

One of the big chocolate factories even has a 30-foot chocolate fountain!

I think I'll doggie paddle in it for a while.

No more time for that – my humans are back on the train. I wonder where we're going next?

I love looking out at the beautiful Swiss countryside. Wait, that sign just said Welcome to Germany - are we going to rocket around GERMANY? Auf Wiedersehen (good bye in German) for now! *To be continued...*

Fast Facts - Germany:

- *Is located north of Switzerland.*
- *Is nine times bigger than Switzerland.*
- *Has about 10 times as many people.*
- *Has one official language - German (Switzerland has four - German, French, Italian, and Romansh).*

Switzerland

Match the numbers to the sites on the next page.

Germany

Zurich
29, 30, 31

Lucerne
18, 19, 20, 21,
22, 23, 24, 25,
26, 27, 28

6, 7, 8, 9, 10, 11, 12,
13, 14, 15, 16, 17
Lausanne

Lake
Geneva
Geneva
1, 2, 3, 4, 5

What's on The Map

Geneva:
1. Water jet fountain
2. Flower Clock English Garden park
3. Exploracentre science center
4. Natural History Museum
5. International Museum of the Red Cross and Red Crescent

Lausanne:
6. Ouchy Promenade
7. Old Harbor
8. Olympic Museum
9. Cathedrale de Lausanne
10. Cite hill
11. Market staircase
12. Restaurant with fondue
13. Place de la Palud
14. Lausanne City Hall
15. Fountain of Justice
16. Grand-Pont
17. Church of Saint Francois

Lucerne:
18. Old Town Lucerne
19. River Reuss
20. Lake Lucerne
21. Mount Burgenstock
22. Mount Pilatus
23. Mill Square
24. Spreuer Bridge
25. Chapel Bridge
26. Swiss Museum of Transport
27. Port of Lucerne
28. Swiss Alps

Zurich:
29. Lake Zürich
30. Limmat river
31. Chocolate Fountain

German Phrases

German is the most widely spoken language in Switzerland. Out of the country's 26 cantons (sort of like states), 19 are German-speaking.

English	German
Hello	Hallo
How are you today?	Wie geht es dir heute
My name is	Wie heissen Sie
Can you help me	Kannst du mir helfen
Where is	Wo ist
I am lost	Ich bin verloren
I love to rocket around	Ich liebe es, durch die Gegend zu rasen
How do you say in English?	Wie sagst du das auf Englisch
Good bye!	Auf Wiedersehen!

French Phrases

The French language is spoken in the "Suisse Romande" – the western part of Switzerland. And includes the cantons of Geneva, Jura, Neuchâtel, and Vaud.

English	French
Hello	Bonjour
How are you today?	Comment allez-vous aujourd'hui
My name is	Mon nom est
What is your name?	Quel est ton nom
Can you help me	Pouvez-vous m'aider
Where is	Où est
I am lost	Je suis perdu
I love to rocket around	J'aime faire des fusées
How do you say in English?	Comment dites-vous en anglais
Good bye!	Au revoir!

Be a Rocketarounder!

--Read *Rocket Around Switzerland* AND do activities on rocketaround.com - Join Rocket in building your brain through adventure, imagination, and finding new ways to have fun!

--Let Rocket's human family know: Where should Rocket and his humans go next? Where would your dog want to rocket around with Rocket? (make sure your mom and dad are okay with it first). Email your ideas to lee@rocketaround.com

If you did these things, GREAT JOB!
You are an official Rocketarounder...
welcome to the Club!

Rocket Around
Switzerland

I'M A ROCKETAROUNDER!

I build my brain through:

-Adventure

-Imagination

-Finding new ways to have fun!

44

The Humans + Rocket

Rocket is real, and he lives with his awesome neurodiverse family (his words, not ours) in Alexandria, VA.

They love adventure and traveling, reading, writing, sports, music, chess, anime, chewing sticks and toys, and sleeping.

They hope you enjoyed this book and that you'll read the next one!

More from Rocket Around

Books:

Rocket Around Washington DC – a neurodiverse visual guide with activities
Rocket Around Washington DC – a neurodiverse storybook
Rocket Around Washington DC! Neurodiverse activity + coloring book
Rocket Around Washington DC Ebook
Rocket Around Switzerland - Neurodiverse-friendly visual guide + activities
Rocket Around Switzerland - Neurodiverse-friendly storybook
Rocket Around Switzerland! Neurodiverse-friendly activity + coloring book

On the Internet:

Rocketaround.com blogsite on adventure & life for neuodiverse families

Facebook - https://www.facebook.com/groups/rocketaround

Instagram - https://instagram.com/rocketaroundtheglobe?igshid=YmMyMTA2M2Y=)

Pinterest - https://www.pinterest.com/rocketaround/